Like the Pieces
of Driftwood

by
Jon Francis

Other books by Jon Francis

1. FRAGILE INTERLUDES
2. LIKE THE PIECES OF DRIFTWOOD
3. COLORING BOOK PORTRAITS

($5.95 each)

available from:

JON FRANCIS
P.O. Box 113
Mendocino, California 95460

contents

Like the Pieces of Driftwood

LIKE THE PIECES OF DRIFTWOOD

I found a dead sea gull today.
he was lying beneath a steep sandstone bluff;
twisted and broken,

    decaying
like the pieces of driftwood
and the piles of kelp
  around him.

    And the air hung damp
        and grey.
    And the sea was pounding;
    Constant,
        loud,
            and violent.

And above,
his comrades and companions
still sailed upon the breezes
and soared or' the cliffs,
         the sea,
that he too once had known.

    And his body lay cold in the sand.
    And no one seemed to know,
        or care.
    And the wind grew bitter.
    And the rain began to fall.

And to me, the observer,
it all seemed so lonely
        and cruel.
  (The ultimate reality
  in the story of life)

But somehow,
it was also beautiful:
beautiful in that
    he had come to rest
by the cliffs and the sea he loved.

And because,

that was where he belonged.

IT HAD BEEN SO LONG

I went out to Sunset Beach today,
parked the car in the eucalyptus grove
        and climbed over the dunes
            to the bay.
I walked along the beach
where the sand was cold and damp.
It all felt strange somehow,
                almost alien;
as if I didn't belong,
as if I were a trespasser
    upon some foreign shore;
perhaps because
it had been so long.

And the shallow, creeping waves,
             the foam,
          the retreating bits of sand;
they swam, touching and darting,
                about my feet.
As if to ask,
       wanting to know,
"Who is this who wanders here?"
"Is it friend or foe?"
But then,
it had been so long.

I found our sandy little knoll,
surrounded by the tall, blowing beach grass.
And I sat there on the sand,
and looked out to the sea-
          the sand, the sun, the sea—
                the twisted cypress
             and the fading blue sky.
This was the first time I'd been here
since that morning we'd said goodbye.
And it had been so long.

It was hard at first.
Even as I parked the car
I felt the urge to turn and go.
       But I went on.
I knew I had to.
And sitting on that knoll,
          our little sandy knoll;
at first I could only recall
the days, so many days,
and the nights,
          such precious nights.
I tried to think of what we had said,
but I couldn't quite remember.
I only know that I had loved you.
But then,
it had been so long.

I think I cried a little
                    at first.
But then I knew that I would,
                    at least some.
I guess thats why I didn't want to come.
But I had to break this last chain
before I could again be free,
free to turn and love again
with no binds
                    except-
          the eternal memory.
I had to be free.
And besides,
it had been so long.

I remembered then
          so many years ago;
those years when I was free,
not content, not really happy;
but hoping, searching,
                    and free.
I loved this beach then.
It was the dearest friend to me.
You might have said it was my lover:
          always there, understanding and wise,
                    always tender.
But then,
that was when I was free.
And it had been so long.

I walked back in twilight,
along the beach,
amongst the soothing,
                    cooling sand.
And the shallow, creeping waves,
                    the foam,
          the running bits of sand;
they laughed and played about my feet.
As if to say,
"Why sure, we know you now".
And as if to ask,
"Why had it been so long?"

A PIECE OF A SHIP

I found part of an old sailing vessel today.
It had been washed ashore
        and was lying in the sand.
There was about fifty or sixty feet
of the deck railing
  and part of the hull.

Her timbers were huge-
like the kind that might have been used as beams
        in a church or on a bridge. or supports,
And they were beaten and worn,
with knots and cracks and grains;
  in shades of brown, and blackened grey.
And holding them all together
were ancient bolts of iron;
as long, or longer
than a grown mans arm.

Some were intact—
as when they had first been placed.
And others, (where the timbers had rotted
                or broken away),
    stuck out naked—
      bent and twisted.
And all of them were pitted,
                and rusted,
                and dead.
And they stained the wood around them
in streaks of russet-yellow,
and spreadings of orangish decay.

It was just an old, derelict piece
    of a long forgotten ship;
but still it seemed proud and supple,
  even as it lay there
                alone in the sand.
And one could gaze upon it
and wonder at the times and adventures
      that it must have known—
the joys and the dangers
  that it must have seen;
and the beauty that once,
it must have been.

I sat there on a rock
  through the late afternoon-
      'till almost dark.
And I thought of those who had loved her:

I thought of the men who had built her-
of the days and months and years they had spent,
and of the pride they must have known
      at her completion.
And I thought of those who had sailed her-
those who had laughed and loved;
    dreamed, struggled, and cried—
  perhaps even died-
beside her.

And I sat awed by the magnitude
and the essence before me.

These few timbers;
      and these rusted, twisted bolts
was all that still remained
of the lives of men,   long since gone.
And soon they too would be gone.

And then there would be nothing.

And I fully realized in that moment,
  how very temporary each of us are;
and how short lived-
        how soon to disappear;
are the things that we build or possess;
  or strive, or fight, or die for.

And I hoped within
that their days had been rewarding and peaceful
and that their lives had been happy.

And the evening, and the sea, and the sky
                were grey.
    And there was no wind at all.
And the timbers, and the bolts;
and the lives and dreams and memories,
lay silent in the sand.

And it began to rain,

and I turned and walked away.

FOR DOLLY HOLLINGSWORTH

The Big Sur coast is cold.
The winds blow damp;
   the light is grey
  and the fog is constant.

I wander across the plateau;
through the low, bracing brush—
        the bent, twisted trees.
I stand near the end of a bluff;
lean to the sky
        and breathe,
  to feel the taste of the sea—
  of time.

        And before me
    I see a grave post;
     enclosed by a flowered bush.

I fall to my knees,
wipe the dirt from the epitaph:

  "Dolly Hollingsworth"
  "born May 14, 1964- died April 6, 1966."

  "Dog who flew on the wings of a sea gull"

The fog rolls thicker.
  The gulls cry.
  The seas pound.
I bend,
to leave a kiss upon her name,
      then I turn
    and walk back-
feeling within
  some overwhelming perception of beauty,

knowing some whisper of envy.

WESTBOUND JET

You fly so very fast-
leaving behind streams of vapor,
      people and places;
leaving behind
           almost time.
         (TOO fast even for time.)
And within you people silently wait;
        waiting for somewhere,
suspended, debared, deadened,
in the mad rush to be at a certain place
        at a certain time.

Maybe you'll stop in Tokyo
   or perhaps in India.
And when you stop, wherever you stop,
time will again begin—
  for you and for your hurried people-
again, time will begin.

There was a boy
and there was a girl
    walking slowly along a country road.
The late-noon sunlight sparkled in her hair
and when he looked at her
       he smiled.
They walked slowely, far below you,
     holding hands and laughing
  along a country road.
They walked slowely,
       happily, peacefully,
with time.

Is it all that necessary
to go faster than time;
to make places more important than they really are
and people, or life, less important?

Might it not be better
to go slowely with time?
Would it not be better
to go slowely,
    holding hands, smiling warmly,
peacefully
and happily.

TREAD LIGHTLY

The wind just blew a tree down on the beach.

It was a huge old redwood
and for centuries it must have been standing
by the edge of the bluff
that stood by the sea.

In its time
it had seen the coming and going
                        of so many things.
It had known the days
when the land was quiet and peaceful—
the days before the coming of man.

It had watched the Indians
        that passed by its trunk—
listened to their stories and songs-
knew their lamentings and rejoicings.

It had seen the coming of the white men
with their ships so graceful and proud,
        their egos and self-righteousness—
            their cruelty and foolhardiness—
and their christian god.

It had witnessed all that had passed before it
from the beginning of silence and harmony
to the present
                    of chaos,
        pollution and insensitivity.
And through it all
it had stood silent—
    only watching,
                knowing,
        and remembering.

But with the years
the winds had blown,
    the seas had pounded,
        the rains had fallen,

and the earth around it slowly loosened
and sank away to the sea—
leaving its roots unsupported—
gradually more exposed and barren.
And then, when it could resist no longer,
it had cried out in torment and agony
as its roots were wrenched from the earth
and it tumbled down to its death.

And there it now lies,
        still quivering—
    twisted and broken—
in the sand
at the bottom of the bluff.

Theres not many things that stand taller;
nor are more solid or older or stronger
than an ancient old redwood.

And while I sat pondering
  all these thoughts in my mind,
a whisper seemed to come drifting—
            come drifting from behind:
from out of the earth
  or from out of the sky
    or from out of the sea—
or maybe it came from all of them at once;
it was impossible to tell.
And it said:
"Tread lightly my little young friend,
for you,
    like this redwood—
like each flower and animal and tree
are as temporal and fragile
as the bubbles that foam
by the edge of the sea.

Live only for each day
and make it as complete and meaningful
     as you may—

for life is a delicacy,

   and duration—
a continuous uncertainty.

JUST HE AND SHE
AND A DOG NAMED "FREE"

The winter now had gone away.
And wooded steeps, and grassy slopes
              lay full and green
beneath the sun.
And there on top a mountain side;
  between the sky,
          the blue,
            the sea,
sat he and she
and a dog named "Free".

They'd come from the south—
                t'were heading north;
to learn what might
be found or seen.
Just gypsy rovers,
          one two three;
just he and she
and a dog named "Free".

Their needs were few,
their wants were meager:
just food and drink,
          and clothes and shelter;
  some sky, some sun,
    some joy, some peace;
a touch of green,
                a glimpse of sea—
and he and she
and a dog named "Free".

And so we met,
  and so we parted,
along the top of a mountain side.
And still they live,
and still they roam,
in distant lands
        and places seldom known—
always together;
          content and happy;
just he and she
and a dog named "Free".

HUMMING BIRD

Swoop
        and stop.
Now pause and flutter,
     to test the taste
     of one small flower.
Or hop, or jump, or dart away
to test the taste
of just one other.

Then off you dash
     some other place,
to swoop
        and stop.
to pause and flutter,
to test the taste
of some distant little flower.

How grand your life
would have to be
to spend each day
    just humming free;
to swoop
        and stop,
to pause and flutter,
    to kiss the lips
    of maiden flowers.
Then dash, or dart, or jump away,
      to kiss the lips
of all the others.

AND WHEN I DIE

It seems that almost everything today
  is becoming too commercialized.

Christmas has grown from a simple
                    religious rememberance
to a colossal economic absurity.
Secluded mountain resorts are being transformed
into neon cluttered urban replicas.
Camping out is a 20 x 30 foot
          denuded piece of (nature?),
  sandwiched inbetween a hundred other
    20 x 30 foot denuded pieces of nature—
glossily occupied by a myriad of 8' x 16'
shinny tin and plastic
          weekend trailer homes;
(totally self-sufficient);
   including:
T.V. antennas,
  dishwashers,

synthetic wildlife sounds,
and all the crowding,
                    cramping,
noise, neurosis, and pollution
so common to other blighted areas.

Our lives have become balanced
upon the turn of a dollar.
  And so also has death:

        from shrouds to pine boxes,
        and pine boxes to gingerbread coffins—
                    velvet, satin,
                and superflous ornamentation—
        guaranteed to keep the dirt out
            for 500 years;
        complete with various budget plans,
        from "instant finance"
        to "pay now, go later" schemes.

Through the days that I live
I'll strive for a minimum
                of rubbers and replicas,
            and plastic-type phonies;
and pray for deliverance
from regimented gaietys
  and simulated realities.

And when it comes my turn to die,
I want no boxes;
            or fancies or frillies,
  or markers of marble.

I want only to be laid in the earth—
  (to pass into dust naturally).

And in accordance with nature;

to be the means
for other life to come.

FALLING STARS

A falling star just fell behind the mountain.

When I was younger,
I use to feel a kind of sorrow
  whenever I saw a falling star:

for it seemed so wrong—
              so futile,
that one of such beauty
should come to so quick
      and final an end.

  I don't feel sad anymore though;
            for I know now,
      that they are not really falling stars.

They are only tiny, insignificant
              bits of matter;
    traveling unobstrusively
    through the emptiness of time
              and space—
until they enter the earths atmosphere.

        And then,
       within our eyes,
they seem huge; and brilliant, and powerful,
as they burn,
disintergrate and disappear.

How often does it happen in life
that small, insignificant-type things
appear to us to be something other
than that which they really are?

Perhaps we should learn
to constantly re-evaluate those things
which seem large
or highly pertinent to us;

for nothing is more senseless,
  nor as needlessly frustrating,
than to be overly concerned
      with things

that don't really exist.

Feathers

FEATHERS

I just found a tiny feather
lying in the grass near the stream.

At first it appeared quite common—
      (a sort of blue and grey).
But when I held it above me
and the sun passed softly through,
it seemed like a miniature prism;
  with hints of colors
   and rainbow spreadings-
too beautiful and too numerous
to name.

It's awfully soft and delicate.
When I brush it against my face,
  I can hardly feel it.

I wonder if the bird that lost it
          has missed it;
     or if he's been looking for it?
He's probably not I guess,
for birds have many beautiful feathers
  and if they should lose one
they usually grow another.

People too have soft, beautiful things—
things like truth, integrity, and sincerity.
But when they're lost,
         if they're lost,
they seldom grow again
like will a tiny feather.

Perhaps if birds
had but a few precious feathers
they would take care not to lose them;
     or if they did,
they would hasten quick
to find them.

GOING ON

There are times when I feel
that my days have been wasted;
for so little can be seen
of the things that I've done.

No business or mansions
        have I built.
No power or fame or fortune
        have I won.
No servants nor land nor gold
        do I own—
nothing to show
that many might say
was of worth.

Then sometimes I look
at a bird or a tree,
    or a flower
        or a meadow
or the blue
of the sea.
And I wonder how much
have they conquered or built,
and how much have they given
to those that can see?

And so I go on
through my days and my nights,
just living my life
as best as I can;

and speaking, and writing,
        and trying to promote
beauty and happiness,
  understanding and hope

within the heart of man.

REMEMBER TOMORROW

You are prettier
than the sunrise
      across the lake;
more alive
than the trees that grow,
      the animals—
   the grasses and breezes
      that blow.
You are softer than the moonlite
and more pure,
      more sincere
than the waters
   that flow
from the mountains.

And you are young:
younger perhaps
   than the dew-drops
on the flower tips—
      as young even
as a morning-glory
before it awakes.

The morning-glories are not sad
and dew-drops are from laughter.
And the sun only rises
        at the beginning of the day.
And the streams only flow
                        after winter
        has gone away.

Forget yesterday.
Forget the disappointments,
                the sorrows.
Live more for today
        and always
    remember tomorrow.
Remember the sunrise,
the breezes that laugh,
the yellows that melt
        in the meadows,
and the streams
        that flow
    from the mountains.
Remember also
        that somewhere
there is love.
Somewhere there is beauty.

Be happy for them
and be happy with them.
And remember mostly
    that you are young;

as young as a morning-glory
before it awakes.

THE ROCK
THAT TOUCHED WITH THE SEA

I just went for a walk down the beach:
far past
    where the road curves away;
down where the mountains
fall straight to the sand,
        and the sand
stops quick at the sea;
and people
seldom ever go.

I met a man out there:
out past the Cape of No Pass.
He was sitting on a rock
that touched with the sea,
    and he was old-
tough and furrowed
    by the wind and the sun;
calm, slow, and wise,
by time and experience.

And I sat there beside him
    on the rock
that touched with the sea.

And the sun moved slowly across the sky.
And the afternoon came
                    and gently waned.
And he spoke of things
that many men have never known
        or seen.

He told of the sun and the winds,
                the currents and the sea;
the beginning and the end;
        TIME;
the fullness of life,
                understanding and sincerity;
the simplicity of happiness,
the joy to be free.

And I listened silently,
        as in a trance.
And seldom did he turn
or look at me.

And when he had finished,
                I left:
back by the sea,
back past the point
        of "No Pass"—
recalling, repeating,
trying in vain to remember
each work he had given me:

    "The sun, the winds;
      the currents, the sea";
      the way of the beginning
                    and the end;
      the beauty and potential
                        yet insignificance
of life;

                and time;

    the value of understanding and sincerity;

    the simplicity of happiness,
    the joy to be free.

PICNIC

for Windy & Daniel

We went on a picnic today;

because it was a warm and sunny day,
and because none of us had been on a picnic
                    in so long
            that we couldn't remember when,
and because it was Daniel's first birthday
and he most definitely wanted a picnic.

Windy got together some sandwiches
                    and a birthday cake
and I brought some ice-tea and cornchips.
And we took the old sleeping bag
        from the van
and went out to the park
                down by the river.

First we played on the swings
                    and merry-go-round's
I had forgotten how much fun it was
to get so dizzy you can't stand up.
Then we went for a walk
        south along the river bank.
And down by the bend,
where the river splits in two,
we waded out to the island called "Jefferys".
And Windy picked some ferns
while I explored the little caves
                along the water line.
I felt almost like Tom Sawyer
or Huck Finn again.

Then, later, we went back
                and ate our lunch
        and sang "Happy Birthday" to Daniel.
And we laid around in the fresh green grass
and watched the butterflies,
and let the warmth of the sun
        sink deep
into our skin.

For a long time there
I just laid upon my back
              with my eyes shut
and rolled my eyeballs
and squinted my face
and followed the swirling colors and patterns
that flowed and twisted
   and merged and melted and faded
behind my eyelids.

And I remembered then
   of when I was very young
and of how much I looked forward
to just a simple little picnic;
and of all the fun I had
walking and playing, seeing and exploring,
   —and especially
just munching a sandwich
on a soft grassy spot
beneath a warm summer sun.

It's still the same you know:
Things don't really change
   unless we let them;
even when you're older,
              or completely grown,
   or have children of your own.

All you have to do
is to let yourself flow with it

like you did
when you were just a kid.

ENOUGH?

The moon hangs low now,
            (directly ahead),
large and full
in the slow-spreading dawn.

And if the road kept climbing,
and did not fall
        beyond the next rise,
we could drive there.

But the road must fall.
          And soon
the sun will rise,
the day will begin,
and the moon
      will be gone.

It's really a sad thing:
to feel the want
              or need
to leave your own home,
    (your own planet);

to wish you were somewhere else;
somewhere where the air was clean,
the waters were pure,
and the food was wholesome.

A place perhaps
where the people were calm,
            gentle and sensible;
and the constant, growing
                    threat of war,
            famine, insanity, extinction
did not exist;

A place where life was pleasant
                    and beautiful,
and the future could be bright;
more certain, more hopeful.

We can't drive to the moon you know
and so I guess
        we'll have to stay here.

And maybe
if the two of us try
to make our earth
        a better place,
it will help.

And maybe,
        if all of us try
it will be a better place.

Maybe,
if all of us try,

it will be enough.

PEOPLE TALK TOO MUCH

Sometimes I think
that people talk too much:
especially when they're saying nothing at all.

They struggle to make their opinions heard—
            trying to impress others-
    to seem interesting, important or pertinent.
Sometimes it seems that they talk so much
  there's nothing left inside
but more talk.

        Listen-
the stream isn't saying anything.
Its just móving through the meadow:
            silently, slowely—
    doing it's thing.
Its not trying to be impressive:
            or interesting or pertinent;
    or opinionated or well-liked.
Its just a stream, —being a stream.
            And its beautiful
because it's not trying to be anything else.

Maybe if people stopped talking so much—
maybe if they stopped trying to impress others;
            or be overly interesting,
        flashy, important, or well-liked
they might come to learn the comfort
of peace and sincerity.
    And maybe,
if they stopped trying to be something else,

they might even start
to become themselves.

Messages of Love

MESSAGES OF LOVE

Sometimes its nice in the winter.
when the storms blow away
                    for a day
                    or two;
when the skies are clear,
the sun shines warm,
            and the days
grow mellow
and blue.

I went out to the beach today
            to listen to the sea,
                    to think,
and to watch the people
who came to spend
a gentle winters day.

A young couple came by
                later in the afternoon.
They ran and laughed,
and danced and splashed,
        and played the games
that lovers sometimes play.

And then,
when the day had almost gone away,
they drew pictures
            and wrote messages
in the sand.

And after they had gone,
I thought for awhile
about going to read them.

But it seemed wrong somehow;
    like peeking in a window,
or looking through someones diary
that they had forgotten
to put away.

The sunset came,   and passed,
and the evening skies grew dim.

The tides began to rise.
            And the winds from the coast
blew the spray from the surf
    back to the sea.

And the pictures,
and messages of love
were washed away.

            And to me,
        and the log I sat upon,
it all seemed futile somehow
and far too temporary.
But perhaps it was only proper
            and symbolic in a way.
For love itself
is so often temporary:

now like the sun,
        vivid and beautiful;
then washed by the tide,
dimmed by time,
    wiped from the sand
and swept to the sea—

            gone,
and only remembered,

like the secrets we whisper
like the messages of love.

PESCADERO PRINCESS

It was rather crudely built
and the wind from off the sea
blew chilly through driftwood walls;
and the sand,
       that was the floor,
was cold and damp.

She had placed an old weathered board
upon that sandy floor,
and often,
     either late in the day
     or early in the morning
she would sit on that board
and watch the sea-
       the endless, rolling sea.
Watching, and wondering, and thinking,
through a hundred sun-bright days,
through a hundred moon-lit nights.

She should have been a princess
and viewed the ocean through castle windows.
She should have worn satin and lace
                and sipped her red wine
            from crystaled glasses.
But as it was
she laughed and danced
in torn denims and faded sweat shirts.
As it was,
she sat on a weathered board
        and loved on a sandy floor;
satisfied with what there was
and only dreaming perhaps
                    or wishing.
            But never expecting,
            never complaining.
Content, and happy
only to sit and watch
the ever-changing moods
                and patterns
of the sea.

If I could
I would have built her a castle
with satin and lace
and glasses of crystal.
And if I could
I would have placed her on a throne
of hand-carved mahogany,
                velvet and tapestry,
to sip her wine
        and to watch
the sea,
the endless, rolling sea.

As it was
and as it is
I can only hope, and pray
                that maybe,
        someday,
someone will.

for Mom and Pop

WE LOVE YOU

You've come a long way together;
from the first dawning of desire,
              respect and love
to the mellowness of time
    and knowledge and familiarity.

And throughout the years that you've known
    there have been differences
                    and disagreements,
as there are today—
as there must surely be tomorrow.

Each of us is different you know,
            (especially man and woman).

The qualities of the sun
are different from those of the moon.
The functions of the earth are separate
from those of the sea.
Yet each is purposeful,
            indispensable;
    unique and beautiful.

Look less upon each others shortcomings
as upon each others merits.
For though they may be difficult to perceive
                        at times;
    they are there,
and most certainly for a reason.

Be not too narrow
            or demanding;
for life is short,
and understanding and gentleness
                are soothing
both for the giver
and for the receiver.

Think of yourselves as two companions
who have come from distant lands
        and who are traveling together—
    each complimenting the other;
    yet never subordinate to the other.

View your accomplishments
                        and your children
with pride,
but never with domination
    or with preconceived expectations.
For they must differ from you,
as the spring differs from the winter.
And though each of them carries a part of you;
each is also, and foremost,
            an individual.
And they must follow their paths
as their souls direct them.

Ask only that they be sincere
    within their beliefs and their actions;
that they strive for understanding,
            happiness, love and togetherness;
and that they respect the rights of others.

Your work has been done in sincerity—
            be joyful.
Endeavor for compassion and unity
for as long as you both shall live,

        and always remember;
we love you-

though different that we are.

                        —your children

39

A WINTER NIGHT

Never before
   have I seen it so dark at noon:
nor so cold, nor so windy;
nor so violent, or gray, or gloomy.

It seems today
as if the sun has departed forever:
leaving the earth permanently
to the fury of the winter.

   I'm sure thats not so;
         But still,
  today it seems that way.

Lets bundle up warm-
         in our scarves and our coats.
Lets walk together along the beach;
and enjoy the freshness
of the winter.

Tonight we'll build a fire,
fix a steaming hot dinner
         of soup and beans;
   and muffins and cheese-
sip some warm brandy perhaps,
(listen to the storm),

and press our bodies close

till we drift away to sleep.

JENNER BY THE SEA

The sun just risen
    melts the night
    and colors the day;
washes the water,
the pebbles, the sand, the sky,
     in brilliance.

Walk to the wind.
Listen to the sea,
    the sun, the sand;
the mellow of the morning,
the whisper of the surf.

     And before you;
see the woman-
stooped and old
    upon her cane:
who walks beside the shore,
turns to look,
stops to think,
   and sits
to ponder,
to understand,
to feel.

The woman;
far older and wiser than we;

who smiles

and says, "Hello".

for Anne Miller

THE LITTLE RED, FISH-NET BEACH BAG

I went out clamming today;
along the western banks of Sequim Bay.
I took the old rusted hand rake
    I had found in the sand
and the little red, fish-net beach bag
  which you gave me;
with the tiny brass rings
and the pull-shut top,
to carry them back in.

And later,
while I was sitting on the bluff by my truck.
watching the late-afternoon sunlight upon the water
       and waiting for the fire to get hot;
I looked over at that little red, fish-net beach bag
          lying across the table.
And I thought of how very perfect it was
for clams, or sea shells, or driftwood;
or anything that one might find along the beach.

And then I thought of you
and the day when you had given it to me.

I was leaving that day.
And you were leaving the next.
And as I drove past your campsite
you called out to me
                and ran up to my truck.
You said, "Here,"
   "I want you to have this."
"It's really nice for picking up things on the beach."
Then you gave me a kiss
and waved goodbye.

I know I'll probably never see you again;
'cause thats the way it usually is
with people you meet on the road.
But everytime I go out tripping' by the sea
with your little red, fish-net beach bag;
                I'll remember that day.

And from wherever I'm at;
           I'll stop
        and think of you.

And I'll send you a kiss.

A LETTER TO MOM

Jan. 12:

It's nearly mid January now,
and although the central coast
             is usually cold and rainy
                          this time of year;
the past two weeks have been almost like summer.

Its been warm and sunny;
and quiet, and calm, and clear.

I've been spending a lot of time lately
      just lying on the beach,
counting the sea gulls-
                   the plovers and dowitchers;
or seeing how many colors of sand
   I can find.
(Did you know that blue is the rarest of all?)

Or sometimes,
I might pack a lunch
and spend the day out hiking;   exploring.

         And then,'once in awhile,
I'll just sit around my camp and read;
            or play my guitar;
   or make neat little presents
      of driftwood, seashells, and dried weeds
for my friends along the coast
and for the people I miss
   back north.

There's a river here,
   that flows by my campsite.
It moves so slowely
that its almost like a lagoon.
Mudhens and ducks play in the tullys;
                              reeds and branchs
that grow by its sides,
and hang or' its banks.

         And in the evenings,
little fish jump for the bugs
   that float on its surface—
making thousands of circular ripples
                     that spread,
                          and merge;
      and fade, and disappear.
And then start all over again.

And there's squirrels and rabbits and raccoons;
and they all seem to be quite friendly.
A few of them even come by to visit
                     from time to time:
   (usually around noon,
         or earily in the evening;);
(right around lunch
or supper time).

Guess they know
I've always got an extra piece of bread
                     or two.

Jan. 14:

Its late in the afternoon now
and a cool N.E. breeze
    is gradually growing stronger.
It's rustling through the pine and eucalyptus
                        behind me;
sending a constant procession of little wavelets
            down the river,
        toward the dunes in the distance
and the sea beyond.
    And high above;
a scattered, drifting haze
is slowely spreading thicker
        —and the sun is going down:
growing vague
    and dimmer.

Have to say goodbye now
and head out over the dunes
    to watch the sunset,
and to check out the clouds
blowing in from the north.

I'll probably be leaving tomorrow,
    (especially if it looks like rain).

Its always kind of sad in a way
        to have to leave a place
just when you're starting to become attached to it.

But there's still a lot of wanderlust in me,
and a lot of beautiful places
I haven't yet known.
(Guess that's one of the hang-ups
about living on the road.)

I'll be seeing you soon I hope;
    'till then,
try to stay on top of it all
        and remember,

I love you very much.

                    Peace and Happiness,
                        Jon.

Look!
The storm is beginning to break.
The clouds are parting
          and the sun
is trying to shine through.

It'll be dark soon.
But tomorrow should be warmer—
perhaps even sunny and blue.

Lets spend the day at the beach.

I know a place
where the shells are as big as your heart
and if you hold them to your ear
they whisper messages of love.

I'll find you the fairest of them all.
And when you hold it to your ear,
perhaps it will tell you

how very much I care.

A VERY IMPORTANT THING

Its a dark foggy night
on the central Oregon coast.

The narrow little streets and roadways
            lie somber and quiet.
And although an occasional yellowish light
gleams silent from behind
      some distant curtained window;
its glow seems vague and remote —
as though of another world,
                  or another time;
   or as of a dream,
      or a memory
            or an illusion—
serving only to make the fog appear more intense
and the feeling of isolation,
   more profound.

The trees rise like ominous shadows
   against the haze of the sky.
There are no stars, nor moon, nor wind;
only the fog—
            the silence,
and the damp, penetrating mist
that seeps through my Levis
   and clings cold upon my skin

I often go out walking in the night,
    especially when I'm in some faraway place.
It gives me a chance
  to get to know a city;
or to feel the essence of a countryside
when there are not the noises,
            confusions,
        or diversions of the daytime.

Its a time to stroll slowely,
                and think—
breathe the freshness of the air,
  reflect upon the day just behind
and plan for the day just ahead.

Its one of the times
that I enjoy the most.

But somehow this year,
  it doesn't seem the same.
Its not as serene—
not as soothing, peaceful and pleasant
        as it usually is;

and I guess its because
I'm still so very much in love with you.

I use to think that love was secondary—
that ideas, and goals, and purpose;
   independence, solitude, and freedom
were far more essential.

I use to think
that I could be perfectly content
with only myself—
               with nature—
with my friends and with my work.

   But I was wrong.

Love is a very important thing—
      (giving love;
            and being loved).
Its more important than wealth or prominence;
or institutions, or rockets to Mars,
               or economic progress.
Its as vital as seeing or hearing,
      or thinking or touching or smelling;
and as primal as breathing,
or eating or sleeping or drinking.

I guess its almost as important
as living itself.

Its just too bad
that some of us never fully realize it
until after its gone.

*In the Spring
or late Fall*

Sometimes,
in the spring or late fall,
a northern wind might blow
driving herds of stormy clouds,
          silent and low,
over the mountains
and out across the lake.

And often,
from between the patchwork of the clouds,
bright beams of late-noon sunlight
                    cast pools of brilliance
               upon the water.
They move and shift
     as do the clouds.
New ones appear
as old ones fade
     and disappear.

Life is like that you know.
There are gray, stormy clouds
                         and also,
          if one looks,
there are beams and pools of sunlight.
One must follow those beams
and if they fade
          or disappear
One must find another,
for there are always others there

          if one only looks.

I WISH YOU HAPPINESS

I tried to call you today,
but your phone had been disconnected.
        And when I called Linda,
she knew only
that you had gone to Mexico.

I knew that you were leaving soon,
but I didn't know when.
And I wanted to see you
                at least once,
        before you left.
But I can't now.
I've waited too long.

You've been roaming for a lifetime it seems,
looking for something your not sure of—
existing in some place
you haven't found yet.

Perhaps it awaits in Mexico
where time grows slow
        and one can stop for a bit;
        (think reconsider, and reflect).
Perhaps you'll find it there.
At least I hope so.

But wherever you go,
        whatever you find,
I wish you happiness
and a fulfillment that never ends.

For few upon this earth
have searched so honestly,
                or so long;

and none that I've known

deserve it more than you.

ITS RAINNING IN THE FOREST

Its rainning in the forest.

Its not rainning very hard;
    just a mist-like drizzle.
And sometimes it's so light
it seems like only a drifting moistness
  sinking slowly through the trees.

The rain usually gives one the feeling of sadness;
        or of melancholy,
    or nostalgia or regret.
Its like teardrops, or sorrow,
        or remembering.

But today the rain is different.
Its slow and peaceful—
      almost joyful;
pleasant, soothing, and delicate.

It floats through the grayness—
         shadowing the sun;
yet it does not omit the light.
It settles in the trees
    and drops upon the leaves;
           till finally,
            to the earth.
And each "tish", and each "tash",
and each splash that it makes
        is heard;
yet does not seem to minimize
the silence that prevails.

And the dampness that it spreads
    is subtle—
  almost unnoticeable.

    Come,
  lets go for a walk.

Its rainning in the forest.

THE HAPPY EVER-AFTER

Just over the mountain
and around the bend,
there stands an old wooden gateway;
                     and beyond it—
           a tiny, winding dirt road.
It twists its way through the meadow,
past the aspen trees,
                and off
into the pines.
And 'tis said,
it is the road to the happy ever-after.

So many times,
have I stopped at its beginning.
So many times
        have my eyes followed it
across the meadow,
past the aspen trees,
            and off
        into the forest.
And so many times
                have I sat and wondered
what lies at the end
of the road to the happy ever-after?

And although I've wanted to,
I've never walked that road;
            perhaps because
I've never known anyone
I wanted to go there with.
I've never known anyone
I wanted to stay there with.

If ever it happens
        that I find my someone,
I hope that that road is still there.
                And if its not,
we'll find another.
For always,   somewhere,
if you've found your someone,

there is that road
to the happy ever-after.

FOR EVERYONE

For everyone there are mountains:
                          rivers and deserts;
fields to be plowed,
seeds to be sown·
      hardships and tribulations;
   forests and fences.

For everyone there are difficulties:
             ordeals and journeys;
past sorrows
and future uncertainities.

The mountains before you
             are furrowed and trailed.
The rivers have shallow crossings,
   and the deserts have oases.
Each forest has some clearings
and each fence can be scaled.

      And within each person;
past sorrows can be lessened—
   (not forgotten; but softened),
and future uncertainities should seldom be noted·
   unless,
      and until,
they become the present.

For everyone there is hope.

Believe in YOU.
For without confidence and fortitude
    there can come little progress.

Know the limitations,
        yet also the possibilities
    of life.

Then reach for the goals
that you desire.

Face the mountains with resolution
            and climb.
    (Remember that the assent
    can be just as rewarding as the final attainment.)
Confront the rivers with courage
        and the deserts with strength-
    the forests with caution,
        and the fences with determination.
For though, for everyone there are obstacles;
for everyone there is also peace,
        joy and gratification.

    And for everyone:
everyone that lives and dreams and tries,
        there is a valley—
a quiet, distant valley-
    which can only be reached
by rising above
        and passing over
the obstacles, difficulties, and uncertainities.

Remember that for everyone there is a valley;
that attainment is possible.

and that happiness is real.

SOMETHING AND NOTHING

Once there was nothing.
I saw it.
I thought it was something;
    a rare, wonderful something.

Thinking this,
I gave my everything.
        And then,
        much later,
I learned it was nothing.

I took away my everthing;
    crying, lamenting,
        but still
I took away my everything.

Through it all
    I've learned something.
I've learned that sometimes nothing
appears to be something.
And before one gives everything
one must be sure
        that something

is something.

Love comes abundantly
                    for some.
They've always got a lover
and when it's gone,
                    when it's over,
there's always another
                    and another.
It's like turning on a faucet;
pushing a button, pulling a string, flipping a switch,
                    jumping into a closet
              and finding
              instant love.
Sometimes I wonder
if they really love at all.

I've been in love before.
              Not often.
It's not hard to fall in love.
It's just hard sometimes
to find someone worthy of love
and capable of returning love.
It's hard sometimes to find values,
              discrimination,
                    and sincerity.
But when they're found,
              when love is born,
all the silent years
of searching, of hoping,
of wanting, of waiting,
                    are more than worth
the joy of real loving.

IT HAS TO RAIN

The rain is still falling;
but lighter today.
And the blurs and bubbles and streams
                    that form,
slide slowly down the window pane
and drop to the earth below;
to nourish a flower
            or blade of grass,
and to disappear.

It has to rain sometimes you know,
even though it might be nicer
if it were always sunny.

        But then,
usually the rain doesn't last too long,
                    and soon
the sun must shine again.

Could it be,
that if it never became cloudy or grey,
            if it never rained;
the sunshine would seem too common
and we might not appreciate it as much?

        and like the rain,
the difficulties and hardships
                    or life
are also temporary —
especially if we always confront them
and do our best to conquer them.

And maybe
        they too have a reason.
Maybe thëy are there
to help us appreciate the good times
a little more.

IN THE MORNING

I sat in the morning
and watched the sun
rise slow behind the trees.

And the light grew stronger;
spreading through the sky,
  upon the earth,
    in my eyes.
And my tears,
    that had grown through the night
soon dried
and vanished away.
And I marveled at the sun—
                the morning—
      the beauty and life and wonder:

and I laughted at my pettiness.

REASON ENOUGH

The sun should still be above the horizon;
yet the darkness of the western sky
is almost deeper than that of the sea.
To the north and south and east
the ominous curtain is both solid and thick.
The wind beats unmercifully upon the land,
the trees bend and groan in her wake,
    and the inhabitants are huddled
within their shelters.

The world seems abandoned
and the darkness seems final.

    And there,
by the edge of the surf and the sand;
through the rain and the wind and the cold;
runs a boy and his dog—
    unconcerned, undaunted—
laughing and playing together;
breathing deeply
  and gaily.

Gloom, or sorrow or depression
  are only within ourselves.
They come with lifes storms
    and will stay,
for as long as we let them.

But perhaps we can learn to look over the darkness,
    and to enjoy life;
regardless of the circumstances around us.

For just to be alive—
just to be living
  and breathing
    and seeing—

should in its self
be reason enough.

Cycles

CYCLES

The foothills look old and desolate
   near the end of august.
The grasses are tall—yet dry;
       faded yellow,   and bent.
The creek beds are bare
 and the twisted oaks,
      that stand upon the hills,
seem to be recalling sadly
a time when the year was younger:
the grasses were green and brighter,
the streams were running
            and free,
and life abounded
more gay and fuller.

But the earth knows,
      and the breezes know,
and maybe even the trees know
that it's only the passing of the seasons.
  And that soon
the spring will come again;
the grass will green again,
    and dance and sway
   in a gentle wind.
The streams will run
       and laugh,
and life will be real,
and full and bright
  and happy again.

We are only a part of nature you know
and surely we;
     like the silent, twisted trees;
should not grow too depressed or despondent
when the times around us seem barren
       or lonely or dying.

We must always remember that nature
                and time—
    good times and bad times,
flow in cycles.

We must remember; and try,
    with a little more confidence and hope,
to improve upon the present
 and to look forward
  to the future

and to the turning of the cycle.

ON THE ROAD AGAIN

Its really nice
to be on the road again:
to have left what lies behind,
  to look forward to
  and to wonder
what lies ahead.

Its really nice to be free again:
to have no holds
                or demands;
  no obligations, or time-tables.
Its really nice
      except that this time
something is wrong.

You're not with me.

      And although
    I almost always travel alone;
  his time
    had thought
that we would be together.

The northern coast is pretty in the fall.
The leaves are yellow
   green, orange, and red.
The sunsets are spectacular –
                     unique.
And the beaches are warm—
  yet deserted
             and peaceful.

But I guess that Europe
is also beautiful.

Perhaps I should be thankful
                  and content
that at least for a time
  our paths did cross;
that I met you
     and knew you
          and loved you.
Perhaps I should be satisfied
with what has already passed
and carry no expectations
  for tomorrow.

    Yet still
  I hope that maybe:
when winter has come and gone,
when Europe grows old
                  and common,
when your home, and friends, and loved ones
   seem more distant
      and longed-for

you will come back
and we can be together,

on the road again.

THE HARDEST OF ALL

Falling in love isn't hard,
            its easy,
if one is capable of love
and finds another
        equally capable.
It comes natural,
like feeling or breathing or laughing;
and its wonderful—
      the most wonderful part of living

Its falling out of love
or leaving love
or having love leave you
              thats difficult.
Its hard sometimes
        to go on
      knowing
that love is going
or has gone.
Its hard then
      looking and planning ahead;
and harder yet,
              the hardest of all,

learning to forget.

for Lee

THE CHEESE-PUFF TREES

Its autumn again;
and along the slopes of Hope Valley
the air has grown cool
                    and crisp.
The deer have left for the winter,
and the cheese-puff trees
        are in bloom-
shades of yellow, orange and gold
                    clothe the leaves
        that grow in summer
            and die in winter.
And scattered among them:
    around them, behind them, above them
stand the tier-like curtains
                of evergreen—
the pine, and spruce, and fir.

There are times when I think of you;
but mostly in the autumn
        when the cheese-puff trees are in bloom.
And I guess its because
that was the time of our love.

There are times when I think of you;
                and when I do,
                        I smile;
for though our days were short—
    from the turning of the leaves
    to the falling of the snow—
they were real
                and beautiful.

And I'm glad that they happened.

A THOUSAND SHADES OF GRAY

There are no colors out today;
only the wind, and the rain,
                    and the clouds;
and a thousand shades of gray.

The gray of the sea is the darkest
and the foam on the surf
                    is the lightest.
And gray clouds melt into gray clouds.
And the grays of the sky
meets the gray of the sea.
            All
a thousand shades of gray.

Most people don't like the winter,
and when the storms come
                    they hide inside,
            and wish for sunny days.
But the winter has a splendor
                    all its own.
And although it's a lonely
        somewhat sad time of year,
it is beautiful
in its own special way.
        Beautiful, elegant, and proud
in a thousand shades of gray.

Once there was a time
                when even I
            hid from the winter.
I don't anymore.
Sometimes,
                like today,
I might sit alone by the sea shore;
listen to the wind, and the waves
and taste the freshness
        of the mist in the air.
Or sometimes,
I might walk across a meadow
        or through a mountain forest,
and listen to the rain-drops
                falling on the leaves,
or watch the foggy, passing clouds
filter through the trees.
        Watching, thinking, and listening
to a thousand shades of gray.

And even in the winter
wonderful things can happen:
things like life
and flowers that start to grow,
                trees that start to bloom
        and streams that start to flow,
even things like love
            remember?
I met you on a day like today;
walking alone in the rain,
        the fog and the mist.
Walking alone
through a thousand shades of gray.

WITHOUT YOU

It's quiet now,
          because its earily
     and the dawn has only begun to come.
And though the birds are calling
and the stream is running,
          still its quiet.
There are no people
or people-type noises—
only the meadow,
the grasses and flowers
          thick with dew,
the trees that surround,
the mountains above-
                         beyond,
     and the stream
that gently meanders through.

          And somehow
it all seems to be waiting—
waiting for the day you will come again:
the day of your singing;
     your laughter, your beauty, your oneness--
and people will gather
          and dance, and love,
and be joyous again.

It all seems to be waiting—
     dormant, suspended, inanimate;
without the music,
without the band,
without the fullness that it once knew.

It all seems to be waiting,
                    incomplete

without you.

SOMETHING TO LOOK FORWARD TO

It was almost like Santa Cruz again:
the sun was shinning
        and a breeze was blowing;
and in the air
was the smell of green, growing things--
                the singing of birds
            and the coolness of spring.
        And a day; a beautiful, free,
            unhurried day
was just beginning.

But mostly,
        what made it like Santa Cruz,
was that we were all together;
                the four of us,
            for the first time,
in such a long time.

I guess I thought
that I would never see you again;
                    at least
not so far from the coast;
        the sandy beaches
            and the gentle,
beach-type people.

But people meet
        and they drift apart.
And if their meeting was pleasant;
if their time together—enjoyable;
            someday, somehow,
they will meet again.

I know now
that we will meet again—
                    often.
And I can smile.

I have something wonderful
to look forward to.

THE TALLAC SHACK

Once it stood tall and proud.
The windows were large
        and the bright California sunlight
filled each of its many rooms;
from morning—
    till late in the night.

        And in the summers,
        when the evenings were long,
one might sit on the great front porch:
gaze through the fir
            and Jefferson Pine,
    to the lake
    and the mountains behind;
watch the sun disappearing,
    the shadows spreading,
and the stars arising.

And probably,
        in the winter;
when the sun left earily
    and the winds blew bitter
    and the snows fell heavy,
there were chairs of velvet
with cusions of cotton—

    chairs like clouds
that one could sink into,
        lay back
        and relax in,
    to stare 'cross the hearth
                    at the fire
        that blazed in a red brick fireplace.

And there was peace
and comfort, and warmth.

And the people that lived there;
          were good people.
They worked hard for what they had.
And they believed in what they were doing.

They lived in the homes they had built,
ate the food they had grown,
    and cherished the earth
                and the life
that they owned.

The house is gone now;
as are those that lived there.

Only the boulders,
        that were the foundation;
  some broken pieces of china,
  a few rusted utensils,
and the ruins of the fireplace
still remain.

And where once there were polished floors;
        imported rugs, chandeliers and rocking chairs;
there now grows the pine and manzanita.

And where once there was laughter,
  and life and contentment and love;
there are now only mosquitoes,
evening breezes,
      and the cries
of distant birds.

I'll give you this brick
   that once laid in the hearth,
this rusted old spoon
that once was piled high
     with buttered peas,
   and this broken piece of china
that had come from England
and sat behind clear glass windows
in a varnished mahogany cabinet,
          and that once;
                   to someone;
had been the most precious possession
of all.

   And if you like,
we will call it our house—
"Our Tallac Shack":

because of the meaning it holds for us,
because we love it;
          perhaps as much as they,

because we found it together,

     and because

I think they would have liked it.

KNOWING ONLY

I'm back again,
          and I know
that I told you I would be.
But I also told you,
            that this time,
I would never leave.

I realize now
that I must leave-
          perhaps often.
And maybe tomorrow,
      or soon,
I will be gone.

But wherever I go
and however long I stay,

      I will miss you.

And whenever I can,
as long as I can,
as often as I can,

      I will be with you.

Will you still want me?
Can you understand?
And will you wait for me,
         knowing only
that I love you?

THE LONELIEST TIME

There is only silence today
               and stillness:
     not a ripple on the water,
     not a breath
             or breeze
     in the air.
And the clouds that lie low
     are motionless
and dark and gray.
And it's quiet:
     no birds are singing
             or flying,
     no pines are rustling.
And the chipmunks and the ants
          are gone.
And a growing coldness
             lies heavy
     in the evening air.

The silence deepens
and the stillness thickens.
And all nature awaits
     the inevitable northern winds,
     the bitter biting cold,
     and the deep, rolling
          desert of snow.
She awaits
the now long,
          overdue,
time of winter.

For everyone
     there are lonely times:
that time between the end of an old love
          and the beginning
     of a new one,
or that time in the evening,
between dark and sleep,
when one is alone
          with only themselves
     and their past memories.
But perhaps the loneliest time
is that time
     in the twilight of the year;
that time
between the end of summer
          and the coming
of winter.

'TILL THEN

The northern wind has finally come
and with it the howling,
                    and rattle of shutters.
Tonight the snow will fall.
Tomorrow the winter will have begun.

I've never spent a winter without you.
I guess I never thought
        that I would.
I guess I thought,
            (like all lovers)
that this time
there could be no end.
But you're gone now
and the winter has come.
        And for me
it is dark
and the night has begun.

Someday,
            sometime,
perhaps tomorrow
the spring will come,
the sun will shine,
the birds will sing.
        And someday,
            tomorrow,
the snows will melt,
the flowers will grow,
and someone will smile.
                    And love
will again
begin.

'Til then

I can wait.